One Heart Consulting

By Cherry Gates

Self Published by Cherry Gates

04/2009

Dedications

This book is dedicated to my daughter's Timesha L. and Shaneka A. Mckinzie, also to my grandson Jaishaun Hyrne. I further dedicate my book to my parents; Donald and Bobbie Smith. To all of my relatives and friends and lastly I dedicate this book to you and you, in hopes that you find words that are motivating, insightful, and encouraging.

"To God, be the glory for all He has done"

Copyright Year ©2009

Copyright: by Cherry Gates, all rights reserved.

ISBN 978-0-578-02006-8

Prologue

This book was written for anyone who can relate, whether personally or by knowing someone who have gone through or is going through similar issues. The poems are written on reality based content. They are meant to encourage, motivate, or comfort anyone who are dealing with or have dealt with similar situations.

I decided to write this book of poems because so many could identify with what I've written and encouraged me to have the book published. Some of the poems may seem a bit extreme. However, that's why it's called reality based. I felt the poems shouldn't be sugarcoated because it would be downplaying the truth.

My poems speak about murders, abuse, suicide, depression, infidelity, aging, relationships, life in general, and many other areas in life. The book was compiled and written in a way which is very understandable and easy to read.

It's over Now, Let it go

It haunts you every day you're blessed to live
Because of the love your parents did not give
With a confused mind and heart full of pain
The benefit of holding on is none, letting go is to gain

A peace of mind, love, and harmony in your heart
From your spirit the darkness and sorrow will part
I know it's easier said than done, but give it a try
To all of the hurt you can finally say good bye

Sabotaging everything good which comes your way
Because, you can't let go of the pains of yesterday
Wonderful things in this life are awaiting you
Yet you'll never know them by doing what you do

Forgive those who've hurt you and set your mind free
It's holding you back from who you can really be
Your past is all gone never to come again
It's over now, allow the turmoil to end

Cherry ©2009

Secrets

Touched in private places that were my own
Afraid to tell, no expression on my face shown
Stripped of my innocence, once pure as white cotton
I often wonder, do you think I've forgotten

Violated many times, it's all kept inside
Now grown I see you, but I don't hide
Over the years on it I've had to ponder
As I sat in silence and sometimes wonder

I trusted and believed I was safe with you
Now I know, there's no limit to what some will do
I could have become bitter and full of strife
Instead I chose to not let it ruin my life

It's long ago, but I remember what you did to me
Although a child then, it is still a memory
I don't hate you at all not one single bit
Who you are, to my grave I'll go with it

Cherry ©2009

Death

We can't buy our way out of it
It doesn't matter if we're rich or poor
The color of our skin means nothing
For one day it'll come knocking at our door

Some were sick and knew they were dying
Others were healthy as far as they knew
Regardless of what the case may be
Death is coming someday for me and you

You may have a little pain in your body
And off to the doctor you may go
Then suddenly dying without warning
When, where, or how, none of us know

It may catch you on the highway
While driving along one night or day
You're in a wreck and it comes for you
There's no escaping death in any way

Someone may be in their bed sleeping
Or outside working in their yard
No matter where we are when it comes
There's no way for us to be on guard

Well known, unknown, it matters none
As sure as we live, we must die
When it happens loved ones mustn't fret
And no need to question why

I have just one warning for all of you
Which is, "get your business straight"
For if it catches you with your work undone
Too late, too late, too late!

Cherry ©2009

Only One

There's no perfect one in this whole wide world
Not one single woman, man, boy, or girl
We all have flaws it maybe one, two, or three
Not one perfect being which includes you and me

Stop walking around as if you're better than thou
Down on your knees you need to bow
To the One, who sits high and looks down low
For He's the only perfect "One" that I know

You see fault in everyone, but no fault in you
So here's something which I pray you will do
Stop treating your fellowman wrong, all over town
You just may pass them on your way back down

You're not perfect today nor will you ever be
Remove the scales from your eyes, so you can see
What you have, who you are, can be gone tomorrow
Leaving you empty, broken, and filled with sorrow

Watch how you treat others, each day you live
Lest, someday you will get back, just what you give
You may feel it or act it, but I'll tell you what's true
There's only, "One" who's perfect, and it sure isn't you

Cherry ©2009

Father Time

Sometimes thoughts go through my mind
As I seem to struggle just to stay sane
Then I catch a glimpse of myself in the mirror
Tears well up inside and flow like the rain

I don't see the person, who once looked back at me
I've gained a little weight and now wear glasses too
There are wrinkles and crinkles were there used to be none
Sometimes I say, "Hey is that really you "

Amazing how we change as we age
Footsteps are slower and can't hardly see
Sag in some areas I didn't even know I had
All I can say is Lord have mercy on me

Cherry ©2009

Chosen

I loved you for so long, but you never knew
Thought of you over the years and secretly longed for you
Your spirit has a glow so bright for the world to see
Capturing my heart long ago with you is where I want to be

I dream of you in my sleep and think of you when I'm awake
You're special to me and a difference in my life you make
I believe in you and our love every day that I live
In love with you completely and all of me I give

My love for you is so strong it brings tears to my eyes
Tears of pure joy, because true love never dies
You're on my mind daily and I carry you in my heart
No matter where I go or what I do, our love will never part

I'm so honored and privileged that you love me too
Loving you is easy, because of what's inside of you
So, I'll be here forever and forever you'll see
I didn't just choose you, for you too, chose me

I don't know where this will go, but I'll go all the way
I trust you completely no matter come what may
Again I'll say it forever and forever it will be
I didn't just choose you, for you too, chose me

Cherry ©2009

Skin Color

Hating someone, because of the color of their skin
When will this ignorance in our world ever end?
No one was born with an innate ability to hate
It is a learned behavior for which the hater can relate
You don't know why you hate all you know is you do
Couldn't think of one thing the person has done to you

I don't care if your skin is yellow, red, black, or white
We are all God's children and very precious in His sight
We may look different on the outside, were the same within
There should be no animosity due to the color of one's skin
We choose our partners in order to conceive
But, for the unborn child there is no choice to receive

If you didn't have any skin I'll tell you what you'd see
There will be tissues, veins, bones, just as mine would be
If you cut yourself in any place you'd still bleed red
It doesn't matter if you're alive or if you're suddenly dead
Our hearts and lungs all work the very same way
I hope you understand what I am trying to say

You, can change this hatred you were taught as a child
If for a moment you took the time to think for a while
A person shouldn't be judged by the skin they bore
If I know nothing else this is one thing I know for sure
Stop the nonsense and the ignorance which you display
There's nothing we can do we were all born this way

It's so ignorant to hate someone, because of their skin
Who the person really is comes from deep within
Just take a moment to think about what I've said to you
Quit partaking in racism, because it's so wrong to do
If you see your fellow man or woman around town
Stop the nonsense and be kind, lay the racism down

Cherry ©2009

Together We Can

Many hope and pray while living in fear
So for all who will listen please lend an ear
Not only an ear please lend a hand
To cure all diseases across the land

Why spend millions on fancy homes and cars
Why spend billions to find signs of life on Mars
Why spend trillions on missions to the moon
While people are dying, morning, night, and noon

Trillions are spent during Election time
While research isn't making one single dime
Not saying Election time is not an important act
But nothing tops saving a life, it's a true fact

Our Country is "the land of opportunity" we say
So let's stand as one on this issue today
Finding a cure for diseases all over the world
Saving the life of some man, woman, boy or girl

Give your money, time, and commitment at all cost
So to terminal diseases no more lives are lost
It doesn't matter what you give, as long as you do
For the one life you save, may belong to you

Cherry ©2009

Discrimination

We're still fighting a racial fight
Which is plain ignorant and just not right
Hating on the basis of skin color is so wrong
And I am tired of singing this same old song
We all have red blood in our veins so we can live
To sustain life, each other's blood we get and give
Yet we still can't live in peace and harmony
Some people are too ignorant to let the past be
A person's skin color shouldn't make you mad
Get to know the person instead of treating them bad
It's dumb to hate because of the color of skin
For skin color will not matter at all in the end
Despite of your race you came from dust as did I
Back to dust we all shall return whenever we die
The only difference is the color of our face
Still, we all must die and someday leave this place
Stop hating because of the color of one's skin
It will not save or separate us in the very end

Cherry ©2009

Infidelity

Why did you choose me and say "until death do us part"
When you knew you didn't mean it from the very start
A big liar is what you are and it has gotten old
You're always lying to cover the last lie you told
Women call your phone all times of the day and night
It's wrong as hell and nothing you've done is right!

You had the nerves to tell me, how "you love me so"
Your actions only told me it's another lie you know
When I questioned you about cheating you told another lie
Your bags are packed liar and it's time to say goodbye.
I hope she has a place for you to lay your head
You're out of here, because to me you're dead

I don't blame myself, because I was very good to you
You're a cheater who couldn't stop doing what you do
Running around in and out of other women doors
Remember, the next woman hurt could very well be yours
Meaning; your daughter, sister, or even your mother
By some dude like you, who you call your brother

This is about a man, but goes for cheating women too
There's no honor or respect in what cheaters do
The next time you cheat, think if it happened to you
How would you feel, what would you say, or do?
To those who are going through "you can make it,"
You deserve better and don't have to take it

Cherry ©2009

Once Broken, Now Free

Been sitting for hours as I scream and shout
Thinking of my past and the things I'm mad about
I'm numb and can't move although I need to try
All I feel is pain so I just sit here and cry
My life has been in shambles for so many years
Isolated and alone I've cried many tears
My parents showed me no love from the start
I became an angry adult with a dark cold heart

Going through life mean and not caring at all
On my knees it was on Jesus, I started to call
First time calling on Him, I called with all of my might
I felt an unexplainable feeling, although no one was in sight
So much serenity and peace suddenly come over me
I had given my life to Christ at that moment you see
I heard, "cast your cares on me for I care for you"
Dear hearts, if you're hurting this is what you should do

You may be in the darkness, but please seek the light
He, who sits high and looks low, will make it alright
Don't go through your life living in your dark past
The love God gives is an unconditional that will last
If you don't know Him, please get to know Him today
I'll guarantee you undoubtedly He will show you the way
I promise your life will never be the same again
For God is there for you always, until the very end

Cherry ©2009

Seed Donator

A seed donator, is what you were and all you are to me
There's absolutely nothing more in you I could possibly see
I love you because I have too, "in the name of the Lord"
Truth is, loving you in any way for me is way too hard
You're part of the reason as to why I am here today
Yet, to me or to my life you didn't contribute in anyway
You didn't just leave mom, you left us children too
There's no excuse for what you did or all you didn't do
As our dad you walked out and gave us nothing at all
It didn't seem to bother you for you didn't even call
Mom never said anything bad about you to anyone of us
She went on to raise us without any regret or fuss
I want to thank you for acting as if we were such a bother
It, opened the door for a man whom I call my father
He stepped into my life when I was only six
Hearts you had broken he certainly helped fix
He taught me to tell time and was always there for us all
Even sick in the midnight hour he was at my every call
A dad can be any man who donates reproduction seeds
A father is one who supplies all that a child needs
If you died, I'll go to your funeral, but I wouldn't cry
I'll look right down at you and simply say "goodbye"
You didn't help feed, shelter, or protect me from danger
Although I know who you are, to me you're just a stranger
There would be no need to cry or any need to be sad
All I would see lying there, is a "dead" beat dad

Cherry ©2009

Try Him Today

There's someone who can help you when things get hard
But first you must believe in the "Almighty" Lord
He will be there for you in your time of trouble
Call on His name He'll be there on the double
Don't call Him just when you're down, troubled, or sad
Call on Him in the good times as well as the bad
Believe in yourself, but believe in Him too
For all He wants is what's best for you
Some would rather continue to put their faith in man
Despite the destruction man has caused across the land
God will love you despite of who you are or what you do
His love is an unconditional love which is so true
If you don't know Him, please get to know Him today
On Him you can lean and depend in every way
But if in man is who you will continue to put your trust
Then for your soul I'll pray when you turn back to dust

Cherry ©2009

Some Man Better Than No Man

I know some of you won't like the words I will relay
However I must be honest and write about it today
I'm flabbergasted at women who settle for any ole man
One who falls for anything and for nothing he will stand
A man who does nothing all day, but sit and take from you
He'll always be as such because you've allowed him to
The fault lies with the woman and is hers to call her own
Got a man who act as a child, insisting he is grown

He sits around playing video games not contributing at all
Too lazy to help you out even if you happen to call
Many women make excuses saying "he's their kid's father"
Yet he provides nothing at all and is a dead-beat bother
A man is someone who works and not mooch off of a woman
Many women are allowing it today until it's now quite common
Why do you settle for someone who does nothing for you?
A lot of woman claim it's because he's good at doing the do

He may be good in bed, but it's certainly no reason why
A woman should enable a lazy good for nothing guy
Some of you say "a man is just too hard to find"
To be with one such as this, you have lost your mind
Then, some of you say, "oh how I love him so"
It shows your immaturity and you need to let him go
The worst thing women say and some say it with balls
"I would rather have some man than no man at all"

Woman to woman, my intentions aren't to be mean
But you really need help with your self esteem
That sorry excuse for a man you have is so very lame
There are men out there who would put him to shame
It's your decision to choose if you'll continue living this way
If you do don't expect change he'll be the same as yesterday
I pray you understand from my heart these words are sent
Set standards for yourself or a bum is what you'll get

Cherry ©2009

Words

Words are formed early in every child's walk
Tainted by those around them by debilitating talk
"Sticks n stones may break my bones, but words will never hurt"
It's a big lie because words can make you feel like dirt
Not only do they hurt, they've destroyed people's lives
Starting with abusive parents ending with husbands and wives
But, I've come to tell you something and this I know for sure
You no longer have to be bound by those words anymore

People, in general will hurt you, which includes family too
What you think determines how those words will affect you
So take it from me and I say it from the bottom of my heart
Be strong and from your mind allow those words to depart
It's all about loving yourself, despite what others may say
No matter what or who, people will talk anyway
One thing about individuals in this world for which we live
They can't take away your power if it you do not give

Cherry ©2009

Dark Spirit

The past for some is like a blanket of security
People carry it around as if it really should be
A part of their everyday lives as they go along
Lost and hurt re-playing the same sad song
The past is just that; it doesn't hold on to you
You hold on to it and it ruins everything you do
It's the past for a reason and it's behind you today
No one has to live with the pains of the yesterday

I know you feel it's easier said than it is done
Though it may be true, your battle can still be won
It's up to you, to set yourself free from your past
If you never let it go the pain will always last
No matter what happened, how horrible, or how bad
You must let it go and not continue to be sad
Stop carrying around the pain for the benefit is none
Your past can't be re-lived it's over and done

Forgive those who've hurt you, then forgive yourself too
Your past is gone forever and it holds nothing for you
You hold yourself back because you keep looking behind
Because of a darkened past which continues to bind
Binding you up in the present filled with nothing but pain
Sabotaging everything good, as if you've nothing to gain
I pray you find the words in this poem to be true
Dear, you deserve the best and it's waiting for you

Cherry ©2009

The Suicidal Mind
Someone once told me suicide was a selfish act
Now I know firsthand it's indeed a true fact
People tried to help, but you turned them all away
You didn't want to listen to what no one had to say
Withdrawing into your own world you shut everyone out
Not wanting to tell anyone what your turmoil's were about
A lot of your problems stemmed deep from your past
You wouldn't let go, so with you the thoughts did last
I know sometimes in life things can get very tough
But you can make it through, even when it's rough
No matter who you are or where you may be
Suicide isn't the way to set your troubles free
Despite of all the help you still wanted to die
Leaving those left behind to ask the question why
Selfish thoughts and to the future you did not look
If you'd thought at all your life you wouldn't have took
What devastation and shock to find you motionless
Lives turned upside down and filled with unhappiness
Suicide sends a message and it's one which is sad
Because you made it an easy way out when things got bad
None of us is exempt from problems of this world today
That's why I wrote this poem because I wanted to say
Life is a precious gift which was given to us for a reason
Embrace it while you live if only for a season
There is this old saying about suicide which is true
So take very serious what I'm saying just for you
Suicide is a selfish act, from thoughts of pure pollution
"And it's a permanent fix for a temporary solution"
If you feel you just can't seem to find your way
Fall quickly down on your knees and began to pray
Ask the Lord to help you and mean it from your heart
Then turn your troubles over and from you they'll depart
If in Him you don't believe, it's a personal choice if you do
I just pray from my heart, someone can help you through
I'm trying to make a point today for you at any cost
Not another life to suicide, do I want to see lost
I know most times things won't change overnight
One thing I know for sure, is you can win the fight
Battles are our tribulations in life, as we go along
They come for nothing less, then to make us strong
Cherry ©2009

**Voices of the Children
One child may say:**

You wonder why I never listened to you and I will tell you why
As a child you wasn't there and you ignored my every cry
Everything was more important and you didn't seem to care
Different men in and out with drugs laying everywhere
I was hungry having to eat out of the trash and even steal
While you drank up our welfare check every single dollar bill
I remember very well you showed me no affection at all
You never hugged or kissed me nor came when I would call

All you thought about was you and all you wanted to do
Not one time did you ever say the words, "I love you"
No matter how I tried to seek attention, you turned me away
So I embraced the streets who embraced me back everyday
Labeled a problem child to the Foster homes I went
Though all along I was rebelling as a way to vent
Frustrated and full of hate, yet you chose not to see
It's why I never listened, because you never listened to me

Another child may say:

Although you were in the home, you were not there for me
I grew up lonely; you were far from what parents should be
I did everything I wanted and you never said a word
Acting out all of the time, my cries for attention unheard
I was pushed aside left and right, raised mostly by a Nanny
All you ever took the time to do was to roast me on my fanny
Just because we had money it didn't buy what I really needed
Crying and angry it was for your love that I pleaded

You would shoo me to the side and go about your way
I became accustomed quickly, because you did it everyday
As your child you hurt me and I was totally neglected
You didn't think one single time how I would be affected
Time has gone by and many things have changed for you
No longer occupied by all the things you once used to do
Now you want to parent like you should have done before
But, I simply roll my eyes and walk right out of the door

Another child may say:

You were good to me, but I still did what I wanted to do
I often left you in tears, because I wouldn't listen to you
The reason was, because you had nothing to say
Hard headed as can be yet you'd let me get away
I got into trouble; still you were afraid to chastise me
Instead of the parent, you wanted to be my friend you see
Your concerns were focused on not trying to make me mad
So I treated you as the child and sometimes it was bad
I did it because I could and there's nothing you would do
Because you were too preoccupied, with me liking you
When you tried to tell me something, I wouldn't listen at all
I would roll my eyes and say, "you really got some gall"

Another child may say:

We lived under the same roof every single day
Yet we were always separate in every single way
Never eating at the table always in our own spaces
No time spent as a family always going separate places
You two were mad at one another all of the time
So much tension in our home it should have been a crime
Why do parents like you have children is beyond me
So bogged down with your lives you can't even see

No attention, no hugs, and no I love you
More days than not, all I've felt was blue
You both always complained about being tired
If I had the choice as parents you would be fired
Its parents who start their children out in life
Some hurting them deeply, cutting like a knife
Children deserve to have all that they need
Not parents who simply donated an egg and seed

Last but not least:

Some of us will be bad, regardless of what parents do or say
Regardless of how good parents are, we just want it our way
Who will give birth to us no parent will ever know,
A day will come when this child will hear, "I told you so"

Cherry ©2009

Darkness of Depression

In my mind I am lost and have spiraled out of control
I have no desire or energy to reach my goal
I'm like a car driving through very thick fog
Like lungs breathing in hot killer smog
When did it start? I no longer remember when
All I know is that I wish for the madness to end
My world is so black and I can't seem to see
So confused about what is happening to me

Uninterested in things, which once made me happy
I've become bitter, isolated, and downright snappy
I cry all day and most of the nights too
Lost in my thoughts don't know what to do
Bogged down by life with a heart so sad
Can't remember my last feelings of being glad
Sometimes all I want is to lie in bed all day
Not being around anyone, in any way

I know I can no longer go on like this
My life once filled with joy, oh how I miss
It will be a struggle, but I must fight my way back
Shaking this depression to get my life on track
Once unwilling to go on after losing a loved one
I decided to face the loss and from it no longer run
Relying on drugs which pushed me deeper into depression
Thankful for Rehab and therapy I've avoided regression

The past has kept me down with thoughts of doom
Being able to let go has allowed me to bloom
Putting all my trust in man it too caused me much pain
With a stronger belief in myself my power I have re-gained
No longer seeing myself a failure and I will tell you why
Failure comes from a person who chooses to never try
No one is exempt from struggles, battles we all must fight
Every new day we get to live is a chance to get it right

Cherry ©2009

If Walls Could Talk

Oh what a shame for many it would truly be
If exposed by the walls which separates thee
From the eyes of the world which we live in
Exposing to all of society our forbidden sin
Secrets so many try very hard to hide
And in others they wouldn't ever confide
Like, the pastor people think does so right
Abuses his family when no one is in sight
That friend you think marriage is so great
In reality, each other they secretly hate
The neighbor right across the street from you
Beats on his wife until she's black and blue
The smart child you're always bragging on
Steals from you every time he's alone
The doctor in whom many put so much trust
Constantly snorts that white powdery dust
The teacher parents see and think is so kind
Is a straight lunatic and out of her mind
The family you like who recently moved in
Hate you because of the color of your skin
The Chef who prepared all of the food you ate
Spit in it, before putting it on your plate
Your uncle who stops by all of the time
Is a perverted, sneaky, and filthy old slime
There are many in high places doing bad things
Knowing if caught all of the drama it'll bring
Now I can go on for days and days
Illustrating to you in many ways
So people must think before they try to hide
All of the mess they bury deep inside
What's done in the dark will come to the light
They'll wish it away with all of their might
From embarrassment many would surely fall
If the walls, could tell the truth of it all

Cherry ©2009

Life Expectancies

Acceptance is the key
To dealing with life's crises
There are many things we'll go through
About it there's nothing we can do
Like, the baby born with a birth defect
This too we must cope with and accept
Suffering with ailments wanting to be free
No matter who or what, what will be, will be
Mistakes will be made by us all
Don't stay down if by chance you fall
Another tragedy is infants dying in the womb
Nothing is ever promised people just assume
The high horse many people ride upon
With-out a warning can instantly be gone
The food you weren't allergic to today
Tomorrow can affect you in bad way
There are a million of things I could add
Many of which would make you sad
So I'll just close now and say
It's called life and things happen this way

Cherry ©2009

Protecting the Children

Often times our children are afraid to talk
Some are so young can't even walk
If they can talk ask questions and say
Did anything bad happen to you today

If your child is unable to speak
Inspect their bodies do a search and seek
Even with signs we sometimes fail to take heed
But protecting our children is important indeed

We can't pretend it doesn't happen for its reality
Ignoring it will cause them to suffer internally
It happens in families all over the world
To the unsuspecting innocent little boy and girl

I know it's hard for many to believe
It may be tough for many to conceive
Not facing the truth does not fail to make it so
Every now and then ask, just so you can know

Make sure the child knows it okay to tell you
No matter what the bad person said they'd do
As caregiver's we should always do our part
So children won't silently suffer in their hearts

This is meant for abuse in any kind of way
Protect our children all over the world today
You don't always have to suspect to inspect
Pay attention to your child so them you can protect

Cherry ©2009

If Only You Believe

You're very unique no matter what others may say
We all have flaws, yet we're great in our own way
Just believe it and you can do anything you choose
By regaining faith in yourself you shall not lose
You may think you're weak, but you can become strong
Find the courage and the strength to keep moving on
Learn to love yourself and then you can love others too
It is a process, but something you can certainly do
You may see darkness keep going until you see the light
If you hang in there and believe, everything will be alright
Trials and tribulations is something we all must face
It's not about the swift or the strong, so stay in the race
Be strong my sisters and my brothers too
Just believe there is nothing you cannot do
Never be afraid to give it all you can
It will make you a better person, woman or man

Cherry ©2009

Midlife Crises

Middle age is inevitable unless you first die
Your age you may hide, lie about, or deny

It's irrelevant as to what you do or say
It won't change your age in any kind of way

You can pay your big bucks to nip and tuck
Perhaps spend it on a new motorcycle or truck

At this point some people decide to have an affair
Others have accepted it and don't seem to care

Bottom line it's a part of the process of life
There's no need to worry or be full of strife

Face it and embrace it, because it won't go away
If you haven't yet reached yours it's coming someday

Cherry ©2009

Peace in Your Storms

Despite the turbulence our storms can make
Peace lies within for all of us to take
No matter what you've gone through it will be okay
Even if you're going through something on today

Take time to think about the storms you go through
They are to make you strong not to cause harm to you
Storms will invade everyone's life here on earth
They began for each of us from the womb to our birth

You can run from them, but you sure can't hide
So build a strong foundation and on it reside
Then when those inevitable storms come your way
You will not want to give up or run away

Each day you live find time for you
It's so important if this you do
Tired or broken, no matter how you feel
Take time to relax, saying "Peace Be Still"

Cherry ©2009

Simply Say No

I see the pain in your eyes
Although it you try hard to disguise
I see you tremble as you try to hide
All the stress that's built up inside

I see your eyes as you fight back the tears
Desperately trying not to show your fears
Stop trying to pretend that all is okay
Because your demeanor is always giving you away

Carrying the weight of the world in your hands
This is a task too impossible for any man
You walk with your head high, but your spirit is low
It's because you don't know how to say the word "no"

No one in this world can do it all
If you continue to try you surely will fall
Lighten your load and set yourself free
Implementing the word "no" in your vocabulary

Once you've done this, you will feel alright
No more crying tears into your pillow at night
Wonder-woman and Superman were good shows on T.V.
But they certainly don't exist for real in reality

Cherry ©2009

Dry Well

Over and over again
Too much pain
Countless lies
Shedding tears like rain
Far too many years
Nothing but hurt
Abused and disrespected
Left feeling like dirt
Controlling and demanding
Disregarding anything I'd say
Ostracizing me from others
Only having it your way
I gave you all of me
By you I was enchanted
But over the years
You took me for granted
Explaining my feelings
You became outraged
Angry and destructive
Like a animal caged
I asked you to leave
But you said you won't
Swearing that you love me
Actions showing you don't
I don't care what you say
Nor do I care what you do
Since you won't get out
Then I'm leaving you
I've tried for years
To make this work
All you've become
Was a total jerk
You asked can we start over
And this was my reply
"You should of thought of that
Before your well ran dry"

Cherry ©2009

Momma Listen to Me

Momma I just don't understand
How I'm less important than your man
I need you and I love you so
Why you chose him, I just don't know
You told me I could always come to you
To talk to you about whatever I'm going through
Momma, I'm telling you how he makes me feel
And you know what he feels for you isn't real

He gawks at me and tries to touch me too
But nothing was done when I came to you
You're my Momma and you should protect me
You know how he acts, yet you pretend not to see
I should be looking at you as my hero
Not looking at your sorry man who's a zero
Momma he is no good and you know this
You getting rid of him is my biggest wish

No one will help you as long as he's around
All he does is take from us and keep you down
He loses his so-called jobs all of the time
Couldn't reach in his pocket and pull out a dime
He's very messy and eats up everything
Biggest disgrace for a man I've ever seen
Please Momma this man needs to go today
He disrespects us both in everyway

What is it that has caused you not to see?
How this man in our home is affecting me
The example you're setting for me is very bad
It's absolutely wrong Momma and it makes me sad
You're no longer with dad and I've accepted that
But shortly afterwards it's this loser you met
How do you expect me to respect you?
If you keep doing the things that you do

Cherry ©2009

The Stare Down

Let me tell you a story
That is quite funny
About my little grandson
Who is always so much fun
He's very small for his age
But with you he will engage
To break him I thought that I would try
To give him that signature eye
You know the look I'm talking about
When parents didn't have to shout
All they had to do was stare
You knew then to beware
My Mom never had to say a word
That stare spoke loud as words unheard
I've spoken to so many others
Who got the same look from their Mothers
I decided to give it a try
To give him the signature eye
I glared up close so he could see
But, he stared back even harder than me
He topped it off with a frown
As if there was no backing down
I tried to look really tough
Still he wasn't moved by my bluff
It was such a funny sight
I avoided laughing with all of my might
What a picture it was to see
The look he gave right back to me

Cherry ©2009 Dedicated to my Grandson Jaishaun
"I love You"

A Rose in Life's Garden

Rich man, poor man, beggar man, thief
Righteous man or one full of mischief
Sick, healthy, it matters not at all
When the time comes we must answer the call

Your money can't buy you another day
Your status will mean nothing in any way
Your beauty will have no influence at all
When the time comes we must answer the call

None of us knows how or when
One thing is for certain, all lives shall end
No need to beg no need at all
When the time comes we must answer the call

It will be a surprise for many when it comes
Then again, it will be expected by some
No one can escape it, no one at all
When the time comes we must answer the call

Cherry ©2009

Curved Balls of Life

Troubles in life can make you sick and queasy
Leaving you trembling and feeling quite uneasy
When life tosses you a lemon make lemonade
Have a song in your heart to self serenade
At that moment you'll have "perfect peace"
And your troubles for a moment will cease
Troubles and tribulation are a part of life
Sometimes hurting and cutting deep like a knife
If you hold on you will make it through
Regardless of what is ever thrown at you

Cherry ©2009

Excuses

He slaps your face
You coward in disgrace
Screaming silently
As he treats you violently
He constantly curses you out
In your face he spits and shouts
Without one word you walk away
Afraid to speak so not a word you'd say
He does what he wants to do to you
Because it's what you've allowed him to
He calls you cruel names
Then without remorse proclaims
It was you who made him do it
Afraid to say a word, you simply sit
He does absolutely nothing for you
And he's very disrespecting too
You continue to take it all
Still running to his every call
If you don't want to have sex
He rises up on you and flex
Raping you at will
Yet you do nothing still
He does any and everything to you
Because you've allowed him to
When will you take a stand
Against such pitiful excuse for a man
He treats you like you're his slave
It doesn't make sense how he behaves
He brings you down as low as he can
Because he's a sorry excuse for a man

Cherry ©2009

Woman to Woman

Girlfriend you sure make it hard
And a good man you're ignorant to disregard
For there are still some good men out there
You have one, but you don't seem to care
Lying, cheating, doing him so wrong
With him you certainly don't belong
You don't have a clue how to treat him right
Gold digging, tripling, and full of spite

It pisses me to the highest level there can be
That you are ruthless and have no sensitivity
Toward the man who loves you so
Why women like you exist, I just don't know
You make us real women look very bad
You're not worthy of him and it's so sad
One day your man will open his eyes
A light will come on and he will realize

That you're not a real lady, you're only a fake
Then you'll try to do whatever it takes
To convince him your love is really true
By then girlfriend, "he'll be done with you"
For your kind it will be so very good
Because you didn't treat him as you should
You'll sadly run along to connive and plan
Your scheming plot to get another good man

Cherry ©2009

Why Some Abused Women Stay

Confused, abused, can't hardly see
Tainted, damaged, and lost as can be
In her mind she's nothing at all
Don't think she can survive lest she fall

Have children and don't know what to do
Having no money at all to carry her through
No education or skills to go and find work
That is one reason, she remains with the jerk

Her parents, his parents is why she will stay
Too afraid of what they will have to say
Threats on her life and her families lives too
Afraid of him doing what he says that he'll do

Scared starting over will be tough as can be
Many stay out of a false sense, of security
Because of his status, others wouldn't believe
Of all the abuse she often receive

Being told, no one else will want her again
Since she's not as attractive, as she once had been
Manipulated by him into always having his way
These too, are reasons, some women stay

No courage, strength, or faith; she needs to get out
Instead in herself she continues to doubt
Co-dependent with no courage to take a stand
Are other reasons some stay, with an abusive man

Cherry ©2009

Tragedy of an Unhealthy Relationship

The guy I loved was a very violent man
His last attack on me, I couldn't withstand
I stayed too long and now it is too late
Take heed anyone who can possibly relate
I didn't want to die, but I had no choice
Now that I've died don't be sad, instead rejoice

Threatened by him, if I screamed or shout
I was punched, choked, and even knocked out
Fearing the worst on this day I begged for my life
Ignoring all of my pleas, he pulled out a knife
Sticking and slicing as I fell with a plop
Blood spewed everywhere as if never to stop

Out of all the beatings this was the worst attack
I should have left long ago never looking back
The ambulance came for me on this day
Then the Paramedic called me in, D.O.A
It was a shock to everyone that knew of me
Since I told no one of all the beatings you see

I've never in life gotten flowers before
Today I got roses, carnations, and more
So many flowers arranged beautifully
Not for my eyes, but for others to see
My favorites are tulips and I got them too
And a beautiful guestbook signed for me, by you

So many sad people gathered in dismay
Upset and hurt, my life ended this way
Please take heed of the signs you see
It could mean life or death, just look at me
Abuse is something no one should tolerate
Get out at the first sign, later may be too late

Cherry ©2009

Troubles Don't Last Always

Trials and tribulations on every hand
No one is exempt its part of life's plan
Troubles will come and they will go
How long they will last we just don't know
Stop complaining and change the things that you can
You can't change everything, so please understand
You must know the difference between the two
If not, you'll let everything worry you
Life is full of problems, no one is trouble free
The trouble-less people lie in the cemetery
When your challenges of life make you feel blue
Remember someone else has it worst off than you

Cherry ©2009

Excessive Load

Situations can make blood pressures hike
Especially when one's stress level spikes
Stress can be good, but very bad too
Depending how you allow things to affect you

The reasons some have unhealthy stress
They're loaded down with unnecessary mess
It's all about how you perceive many things
As to how much stress the episode brings

Stress can cause you so much unhappiness
I've been there myself this I must confess
There are only twenty-four hours in a day
Good time management helps keep stress at bay

Taking time out just to relax will help too
This is something we all must learn how to do
Stress can cause your health to dissipate
I'm sure to this many of you can relate

It can take both your body and mind
If time for yourself you do not find
No one is exempt it happens to us all
Just don't stay down if by chance you fall

Troubles will come and they will go
This I'm sure you already know
Remain in control of things as you go through
If not you won't manage stress it will manage you

Cherry ©2009

Beating Death of a Child

Not old enough to defend myself from the likes of you
Yet you struck me repeatedly until I was black and blue
Sometimes there was no one around who could protect me
Others times my Mom was there, but she would let you be

How could you do this to someone so small
When you stood over me towering so big and tall
Angered by someone else, yet I would get the heat
Then one wrong move by me and my body you'd beat

You've beaten me time and time, over again
This time you went too far, and my life came to an end
Because of you no more shall I live
And at your hands my life I had to give

My mother knew what was going on
She chose to ignore it now I'm gone
Not wanting to lose him she refused to see
So blind by her heart she didn't protect me

Cherry ©2009

A Ring Won't Change a Thing

You've forced him into getting you a ring
Honey please it doesn't mean anything
All it does is get you off of his back
Because he's tired of hearing all of your flack
Nothing has changed within his heart
He feels the same as he has from the start
Women, I know you feel that you must take a stand
But forcing him into marriage won't help keep your man
If he doesn't want to marry you then you should move on
Trying to push him into it, believe me it won't last long
Yes, it's true; some men want their cake and eat it too
You won't change it, by forcing him to marry you

Cherry ©2009

Soldier's Story

Young and old it matters none
A husband, wife, daughter, or son
Other family members and even friends
Lives lost to a war which just won't end

Killed by IED's and suicide bombs as they blew
They were gone in an instant without a clue
Friendly fire and live fire took others away
Some took their own lives to avoid another day

Hurt, confused, stigmatized, criticized
Often acting in ways no longer recognized
In the combat zone too often and it's a fact
Going home maimed, minds no longer intact

Lost in a their own worlds feeling misunderstood
Would explain how they feel if only they could
Can't seem to find the right words to say
Doesn't think it would matter none anyways

They've been in a war for far too many seasons
Very stressed out and for a good many reasons
So much pain and agony they try to hide
Always praying for the madness to subside

Cherry ©2010

Yet You Remain

He constantly beats you
He criticizes you too
He disrespects you every day
Never having anything good to say
He's very controlling
Always scolding
Demanding as hell
Still, you won't bail

He takes all of your money
Then brags as if it's funny
He has you where he wants you
Still there's nothing you will do
You're afraid of what he may do
Because every day he threatens you
To take your life in a heartbeat
Still, from him you won't retreat

You have no clue what it will take
Before he makes the horrible mistake
Of beating you until you're dead and gone
Still, you won't leave him alone
You know it's only a matter of time
Before he commits the terrible crime
Taking your precious life someday
Still you won't send him on his way

Let him go he's not worth your pain
Get rid of him and peace you will gain
How much more do you think you can bare
Still, you allow fear to keep you there
He feeds on your fear, because he's weak
He knows that your humble and meek
My dear you have to take a stand
To save yourself from such a man

Cherry ©2009

Negative Self Talk

Hateful words you constantly say to yourself
Taking them in as if they are the truth
Destroying all signs of self esteem within
You hang on to the words as if they were a friend

You hate yourself with such a passion
Is it because of others you knew
Perhaps it's due to an horrific childhood
Where you endured things no child should

Is it because of someone you've met before
Who hurt you even more than your past
Tearing apart an already crumbling foundation
Destroying your spirit as with great elation

You've taken it in as if you were a sponge
And others were your showers of rain
Violently spewing terrible words down
Soaking you with pain until you drown

You must make a decision to change things
If you reach deep inside you'll find the means
But if you continue on the way that you live
Your self esteem and power you'll continue to give

Cherry ©2011

The Demon

Snorting it damages your nasal passages
Ingesting it as if it's a delightful feast
Injecting it scarring your skin
Lost and confused no peace within

Smoking it damages your lungs
As you swallow it without any regret
Slowing killing the cells of your brain
While you act wildly as if insane

Day in and day out you do the same things
Not caring about yourself or anyone at all
Living to get that fix any way you can
So out of it that you can barely stand

You're somebody's loved one yet you don't care
How this is affecting your life in every way
Destroying those around you without conviction
As you boldly and selfishly embrace your addiction

Your addiction has become your closest friend
It grips, controls, and destroys you
Sucking all of the life from your soul
And on those around you it has taken its toil

Cherry ©2009

Family Unity

What happened to today's family
They're so different it's upsetting to me
It weighs heavily upon my heart
How families are drifting so far apart

There are mothers against daughters
Falling deeply into troubled waters
Fathers against their sons too
So much confusion, don't what to do

Individuals are hating their own kin
Where's the love, which once had been
One thing families must understand
Divided they'll fall, together they'll stand

It's time families come back together
Together there's no storm they can't weather
Loving one another with truth and honesty
Uniting again the way it is meant to be

Cherry ©2010

The American Soldier

Yes, it is the Solider who signed on the dotted line
Recruiters lying so much it should be a crime
Many didn't fathom the thought of being in a war
Trying to fix other countries some near some far

Failing marriages and relationships everywhere
Yet "Uncle Sam" doesn't seem to care
Many soldiers are filled with unhappiness
Hurting inside and carrying loads of stress

Fighting a no-nonsense war for far too many years
Countless lives lost, loved ones shedding many tears
Suicides across the ranks all over this land
While other soldiers are killing their fellow man

Voices of the soldiers are going unheard you see
Because the Army is filled with too much bureaucracy
Most times it's called a horse and phony show
Trying to cover up things they don't want others to know

The real truth of it all will never be told
Unless the Soldier's stand up and let the truth unfold
It's more political than you could ever believe
Lies and secrets you wouldn't ever perceive

Chains of command with nonchalant attitudes
Soldiers going AWOL so from them they elude
Deaths, affairs, deployments, lies, and deceit
Is the life of a Soldier if by chance one you meet

Cherry ©2011

Haunted by the Past

Dark cold heart
Sets you apart
So much anger and rage inside
Until you can no longer hide
That beast which lies within you
Controlling everything that you do
Losing everything you've had
Which made you madder than mad
Your past has made you a cold man
For nothing right you'll stand
You're always on a crazy rampage
With anyone you'd engage
It doesn't have to hurt like this
But the thoughts you will not dismiss
Downplaying whatever you do
Never thinking things through
Hurting everyone in your way
Because of the pains of yesterday

Cherry ©2010

Intoxicated Driver

Getting into your car to drive away
Many lives changed on that dreadful day
The smell of alcohol so strong on you
Too intoxicated to think things through
One too many is what you had
A night starting off fun ended bad
Too intoxicated to drive a straight line
Reaction so slow you missed the stop sign
Traveling at a high rate of speed
Oblivious to the drunk driving creed
Hitting another vehicle directly head on
Lives once were, now suddenly gone
Unfortunately, you didn't take the time
To avoid committing such a crime
Lives were taken in the wink of an eye
Leaving families torn and wondering why
You act as if you done nothing and it make me hot
And you continue to drink and drive when you should not
You got off, because of a Lawyer who was very clever
Yet you killed someone and they're gone forever

Cherry ©2010

Power of Sex

No matter what, it's engaged in by many
The lives it has ruined and taken are plenty
There are many who are sex addicted
And because of it their bodies are inflicted
With the AIDs/AIDS and STD's of all kinds
Because of unprotected sex and lustful minds
Folks willfully taking the risk at any measure
Just to receive that wanted sexual pleasure
Taking the chance of ruining all they've got
Going home with their privates burning hot
Married or single many still are taking the risk
To perform the act despite of how brisk

Cherry ©2011

The Hand You Dealt

We sat together at the table everyday
In silence not speaking a single word
The desire to communicate is long gone
Blank stares are our words unheard

We're always going our separate ways
Intimacy between us is completely obsolete
The love that we once happily shared
Has been trampled underneath our feet

Sometimes we sleep in the same bed
Other times we sleep in separate places
No more hearing goodnight or I love you
Just dwelling in our own personal spaces

Going through the motions each day
Knowing full well the love is not there
Constantly putting ourselves through misery
Causing nothing but resentment and despair

I can't deny the love I once had for you
Lies and deceit has changed what I once felt
Over the years I tried to make it work
Now you struggle with cards that you've dealt

Many marriages remain intact for the children
Others stay intact for other reasons unknown
But to continue to live in such unhappiness
I would much rather go at it alone

Cherry ©2010

Never Give it Up

People can only hurt you
If you allow them too
They will do any and everything
Because you've been too accepting
Once a person figures out they can
They will, and it goes for any woman or man
Some people will live their entire adult life
For others making all types of sacrifice
Giving up their peace, mind, body, and soul
Letting others take all of their control
Don't give others your power
Because it they will devour
It's really all up to you
What you allow people to do

Cherry ©2010

The Truth Lies Within

Smiles shown on the faces of dark hearts
Cries are completely held inside
Screams which no one can hear
Troubled thoughts becoming harder to hide

Wishing someone knew what you really felt
Too ashamed to let the truth be known
So pretense has become your reality
From childhood to an adult now grown

Stricken with fear that someone will know
The lies lingering behind your kind face
Agony, shame, sorrow, and pain
Dwells within an unhappy place

No one knows the troubles that you see
Every day is a struggle to make it through
Pretending with others won't take away
The painful truth lying within you

Cherry ©2011

Society Gone Crazy

Irrational and don't seem to care
Morals and values are vague
Families are falling by the wayside
Countries stricken with plagues
Lying, killing, and stealing
Taking what doesn't belong to you
Causing chaos across the nation
Still you care not what you do

No shame or self respect
Distorted visions in your head
Constantly fighting the thoughts
Of wishing that you were dead
Filled with constant fear
Stressed out of your mind
No clue as how to relax
So lost, peace you can't find

Commitment is almost a joke
Married folks are doing their own thing
Dedication to marital vows has diminished
Now a wedding ring is just a ring
Many children are out of control
Parents are out of control too
No wonder the children are messed up
They're seeing what their parents do

An alcohol and drug addicted nation
Losing homes, jobs, and families too
But you keep on getting that high
Despite of what is happening to you
I think that we all should pray
People turn from their wickedness
Seeking the blissful comforts of
Peace, love, and happiness

Cherry ©2011

Let Him Go

Let him go if he doesn't love you
Why continue to go through the pain
Angry, bitter, and resentful
Lashing out as if you're insane

He's disrespected and rejected you
Done everything to bring you down
You're still trying to hold on to him
Begging him to stay around

I've watched you slip into depression
Everyday you shed a river of tears
Can't you see that he isn't worth
The agony you've endured for years

Girl you can make it without him
You just have to believe that you can
Get up and shake off those cobwebs
And lose that poor excuse for a man

Cherry ©2010

To the So-called Christians

I'm tired of so-called Christians
Who treat others like dirt
Some hold grudges forever and a day
Not caring who they hurt

They're always downing others
And some have attitudes too
They act so holier than thou
Until they can't see what they do

To these individuals I will say
It's time to take a look in the mirror
Realize what you're doing today
By opening your eyes to see clearer

You don't have it together
Like you think that you do
Everyone around you know
You have a problem, except you

The way you act needs to change
And I mean this very day
For if you think you're heaven bound
Forget it child there's, no way!

Cherry ©2011

You Can't Do It

When you try to do a good deed
By helping out someone in need
It often comes with a great price
Losing yourself as the sacrifice

No matter the good a person tries to do
People often want more from you
Some are not responsible for anything
And to the table nothing they'll bring

They can cause much havoc in your life
Wounding you deeply as if cut by a knife
Finally choosing to make better decisions
Yu begin to act with great precision

No more feeling sorry for them anymore
A change of heart you have to implore
Realizing you've done all that you could
Putting up with more than you ever should

Rendering your power for someone to take
You learned the hard way it was a mistake
Terrible pain you will surely bear
Trying to save someone who doesn't care

Cherry ©2010

Misconceptions of the Heart

You came into my life one day
I was completely swept away
Filled with so much happiness
Then it turned into quite a mess

The person inside of you came out
Quickly showing me what you were about
Angry, disrespectful, and cruel
You broke every single rule

Jealous of every man you seen
Acting downright stupid and mean
The love I thought I felt was gone
I knew I had to leave you alone

You weren't the person that I knew
Who once turned my gray skies blue
You were an imposter from the start
I was blind by my own heart

I followed my heart eagerly
Which caused me straight misery
My life became engulfed with stress
And bombarded with a lot of mess

My heart lead me astray
Spiraling my life into disarray
The signs were there for me to see
But my little heart blind me

Cherry ©2011

Don't Be Afraid

Don't be afraid to move forward
Challenge yourself to do something new
If you don't you will never know
The power that lies inside of you

You can change things if you try
It's really all up to you
Don't complain and do nothing
Failure comes when you do

Don't be afraid to make a mistake
They can make you strong
Don't pine or waddle in it
Learn from it and move on

Have the courage and faith in yourself
It's a necessity that you do
If you don't you will allow
Unnecessary doubt to hinder you

Life is trial and error
Everyday that we live
You shouldn't ever complain
If your all you do not give

Cherry ©2011

Time Reveals the Truth

Many people work hard
To get to the top
Then all because of bad judgment
Back down again they flop

Some Teachers sleep with students
And some Preachers do terrible things
Some Politicians are corrupt and unfaithful
What a disgrace it all brings

Parents sexually abusing their children
Other adults sleeping with children too
Police Officer's committing crimes
What is this world coming to

There are too many professions to name
I could really go on for days
The message I'm trying to convey is
People must stop their wicked ways

Many people get into careers
In thinking that they can hide
That little monster that dwells
Deep, deep, inside

What's done in the dark
Always comes to the light
It can't be hidden forever
When what's done isn't right

Cherry ©2011

Wait On Love

Many people seek out love
In all of the wrong places
Going off of what a person has
Including bodies and their faces

So much drama will overtake you
And you'll learn the hard way
When you're in it for the wrong reasons
Consequences you will have to pay

You'll blindly get involved
Messing up from the start
Overwhelmed with what you see
Due to feelings of the heart

Don't go searching for love
You will mess up if you do
Be patient and watchful
And one day it will find you

By maturing and becoming self aware
You'll be more careful who you choose
There will be no more rushing into love
Cause, doing so you know you shall lose

Cherry ©2010

Flowers While I Live

It never ceases to amaze me how
Some people are hypocrites to the bone
They talk about people when they're alive
Then praise them when they've died and gone

Giving them great accolades
Sad thing they're a little too late
If it were done when they were here
With them you could have celebrate

I would appreciate my flowers
While I yet live you see
They're no good at all in death
Therefore, will mean nothing to me

Cherry ©2010

Violated

An intruder raped you and then was gone
You were devastated and left feeling alone
A mind full of anger and body full of pain
Thoughts twirling so fast you felt as if insane

You scratched and tussled with all that you had
But all it did was made him mad
Afraid to report it, yet wanting him to get caught
Skin under your nails as evidence you fought

Saying he would come back if you told
Words spewed from his mouth hard and cold
Now all you can think of is him coming back
Though vowed to be ready for any other attack

Wondering why it had to happen to you
Feeling so confused didn't know what to do
Washing your body until you rubbed it raw
Remembering his voice, his face you never saw

There are so many tragedies in life
Hurting so bad causing bitterness and strife
No matter how tragic it doesn't have to destroy you
How you accept things determines how you'll get through

Cherry ©2011

Looks Can Harm

Some males and females are immature as can be
Still hooking up with people because of what they see
With all of the nasty diseases people can spread
Some you can't get rid of and others will kill you dead

Yet people are still out there having sex unprotected
Then mad as hell when they have gotten infected
The saying is true, "you can't judge a book by its cover"
Most times it's too late before the truth you discover

It's okay if an attractive person turns your head
But, don't think with your loins use your brain instead
The next time you're tempted by an attractive tease
"If you lie down with a dog, you may get up with fleas"

Not only are there awful diseases to catch out there
You may hook up with a lunatic so please beware
Be more mature in the decisions that you make
Sleeping around could be your last and fatal mistake

Cherry ©2011

Parent's of Teen Mothers

Living with their parents, they're disrespectful too
Don't have a clue about life, but think they do
Most of these girls think they know best
Until they end up pregnant and lives put to the test

Hanging out with the wrong crowd every single day
They do it because you've allowed it to be this way
Having sex with boys when they shouldn't be at all
Soon as she's pregnant he won't answer her call

Pregnant with no job or anything to call their own
It's the price some pay when they think they're grown
Problem is, they're babies too so their parents get stuck
Supporting them both because they can't contribute a buck

There are many teens who fall within this category today
Parents I hope you think about what I've had to say
It's not just their lives which will surely change
The lives of many parents will drastically be re-arranged

Parents, your children do what you allow them to do
If you surrender the control they'll take it from you
When you act as the parent, a child will always know
Who's in charge, because your actions will show

Cherry ©2011

Consequences

When people do wrong they know it from the start
Because it's a conscious decision that they make

Knowing cheating will hurt their spouse's heart
It's still a chance that some people will take

They may decide to stop because of the guilt
Or they may continue until eventually caught

Damage is inevitable to what they've built
Because temptation defiled their thoughts

Once trust is broken in any relationship
It is very hard to build it back again

How would they feel if the table were flipped
If their spouses went where they shouldn't have been

People should think about things before they act
What's done is always a choice and never a mistake

You'll suffer the consequences and it's a fact
If it's a bad choice you choose to make

Cherry ©2010

Bitter Women

It's so sad but unfortunately very true
The magnitude of things some ex's will do
They'll go out of their way to cause a fight
Using the children as pawns just for spite

Acting selfishly, because she can't move on
Bitter that his love for her is now gone
Doing things she thinks will cause him pain
Although by it all she has nothing to gain

Finding out he has someone new in his life
She's filled with even more anger and strife
Giving his new love nothing but drama
Reminding her she's not her kids Momma

Wreaking havoc in every way she sees fit
Ignoring the fact the children are hurt by it
She's bitter as hell and holding on to mess
Causing those around her such undue stress

Trying desperately to degrade the man
Lashing out at him any way that she can
Making the children act out towards him too
Mad, because it's nothing they want to do

Cherry ©2010

Today's Families

They say blood is thicker than water
Once upon a time this was very true
It's now just a saying from the past
Cause families don't love like they used too

They hardly ever get together anymore
Despite the attempts one or two may make
They'll come together if someone dies
But even then most of them are so fake

What happened to the love they once shared
It was a bond held tighter than any glue
These days everyone is doing their own thing
And too mean to say the words "I love you"

Many will act as if they're not related at all
They'll treat strangers better if any they meet
Sometimes they won't say a word to each other
Even when passing one another on the street

The distance between family members is sad
The love they once shared was very strong
Let's pray for families across this world
That they get back together where they belong

Cherry ©2011

Sister to Sister

Some women become so quickly caught up
Blind by love the signs they expel
Many of them choose to ignore the facts
Later finding themselves in pure hell

You have women getting with no good men
They're cheating right from the very start
Everything is there plain for them to see
But they ignore things because of the heart

There are women with men who are pedophiles
They know their history, but do not care
The signs are there like falling rain
Letting them know to please beware

There are women with men without jobs
Acting as if she has herself a King
She gets up everyday going to work
While he doesn't attempt to do anything

Wake up ladies and get a grip
Choices you've made are foolish indeed
For if you keep feeling with your heart
You'll never receive what you really need

Cherry ©2011

Problems Are Only Temporary

I was there for you and you knew this
Thoughts of me were obviously dismissed
It was such a selfish thing that you did
From me and others your turmoil's were hid
I never dreamed you would do such a thing
A lot to pain and suffering your act did bring
Devastated at walking in and finding you
Doing something I never thought you'd do
It turned my life completely upside down
I cried so many tears thought I would drown
Never in life felt hurt like this before
Don't want to hurt this way anymore
The pain was mixed with pains from my past
Had to let them go because I was slipping fast
Into depression; dying from unhappiness
I struggled to free myself from all of the stress
I made a vow to take charge of my life
Leaving behind the anger and strife
I couldn't continue to live life this away
I started seeking for a brighter day
Accepting what is done as being done
So the pain and suffering could be gone
Now I have the desire to want to live
Everything towards change I choose to give
You chose to give up, when things got rough
I choose to keep going though things are tough
Somehow I saw the light through the darkness
First time in a while I feel such happiness
This is my life just as yours belonged to you
I'll move forward no matter what I go through
As sure as troubles come, they will always go
If one learns as they endure, they'll surely grow
No one can get pass troubles if they give up
Because no one is exempt from life's bitter cup
Life has its ups and downs still it's quite contrary
To give up, because troubles are only temporary

Cherry ©2011

Rejoice

Although I write the words it's still very hard
But we must remember the words of our Lord
The Bible says we should cry at a birth
And rejoice when a loved one leaves this earth
It's because of the troubles of this world
Which will affect us all whether born boy or girl
This world is full of both evil and good
People doing things they never should
Hurting anyone to include their family
It's a part of the evil of this world you see
I know it hurts to lose someone you love
No one love them more than God above
It's why He tells us not to be sad
Nor does He want us angry or mad
It's simply a part of the Ultimate Plan
Yet it's hard to accept and understand
So instead of crying when your loved one dies
Remember the good times and dry your eyes
No more pains or worries will they endure
Something we all must go through, for sure
The next time you feel that you want to cry
Instead, rejoice for them and then say goodbye
It's a journey we all must travel some day
We don't know when nor do we know the way
Every day we live, we all die a little bit more
So always live it happier than the day before

Cherry ©2011

Today's Child

Most seem to have lost their way
Disrespecting their parents everyday
Don't seem to have any common sense at all
Most are followers and for anything they'll fall
Those who are able don't want to work on a job
Many are plain lazy and nasty slobs
No ambition or anything to call their own
Always needing help, but insisting they're grown
Many won't listen to what their parents have to say
Wanting everything to always go their way
The Bible says this is the way it will be
And now it is definitely a reality
Many are failing to graduate high school
Because they choose to not follow the rules
Some are so unappreciative until it's a shame
Instead of taking ownership others they blame
Parents end up dealing with their children's mess
Yet their children don't realize how they are blessed
Their biggest thing is to say they're grown
But again, they have nothing to call their own
I can talk about these children for days and days
But I'll simply pray they change their ways
Some of them are grownups who never act the part
Who once stepped on their parents toes now their hearts

Cherry ©2011

ABOUT the AUTHOR

She is a Christian, daughter, mother, grandmother, sister, aunt, cousin, a friend to many, and woman of many gifts and talents. She is a true servant and is hospitable, humble, and hard working. She honors and adores the Lord and gives all praises unto Him. She is thankful for all things in her life and for all of the many trials she's endured. She's educated and has both her undergraduate and graduate degrees in Psychology and Counseling. She loves all people and gives thanks for her family and friends. She prays this book touches the hearts and minds of those who read it.

www.ingramcontent.com/pod-product-compliance
Lightning Source LLC
LaVergne TN
LVHW091318080426
835510LV00007B/549